MW00903509

KILLER ANIMALS
GREAT WHITE SHARKS
ON THE HUNT
REVISED EDITION

by Janet Riehecky

Reading Consultant:
Barbara J. Fox
Reading Specialist
North Carolina State University

Content Consultant:
Deborah Nuzzolo
Education Manager
SeaWorld San Diego, California

CAPSTONE PRESS
a capstone imprint

Blazers is published by Capstone Press,
1710 Roe Crest Drive, North Mankato, Minnesota, 56003
www.mycapstone.com

Library of Congress Cataloging-in-Publication Data is available on the Library of Congress website.
ISBN: 978-1-5157-6265-2 (revised paperback)
ISBN: 978-1-5157-6266-9 (ebook pdf)

Editorial Credits

Abby Czeskleba, editor; Kyle Grenz, designer; Wanda Winch, photo researcher

Image Credits

Getty Images: AFP/Rodger Bosch, 26-27; SeaPics.com: C & M Fallows, 16-17, V & W/Kike
Calvo, 25; Shutterstock: Chris Dascher, 20-21, Fiona Ayerst, 22-23, Martin Prochazkacz,
Cover, 8-9, 13, Sergey Uryadnikov, 7, 15, 18-19, 28-29, tswinner, 10, wildestanimal, 4-5

Printed and bound in the USA.
009969R

TABLE OF CONTENTS

SHARK ATTACK

A great white shark quietly swims through the water. It watches a seal swim nearby. Suddenly, the shark rushes toward the seal.

KILLER FACT

Great whites can speed through the water at more than 20 miles (32 kilometers) per hour.

The shark tears off a piece of meat. It **seizes** the seal in its mouth. Dinner is served.

seize — to take something by force

KILLER FACT

A great white can eat a 400-pound (181-kilogram) seal in about 10 bites.

TOOLS OF THE TRADE

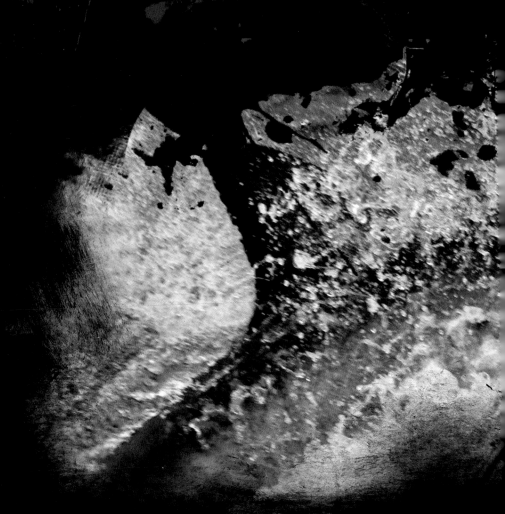

Great white sharks are **carnivores**. They are the world's largest meat-eating fish. They weigh more than 4,000 pounds (1,814 kilograms). Great whites can grow up to 15 feet (4.6 meters) long.

carnivore — an animal that eats only meat

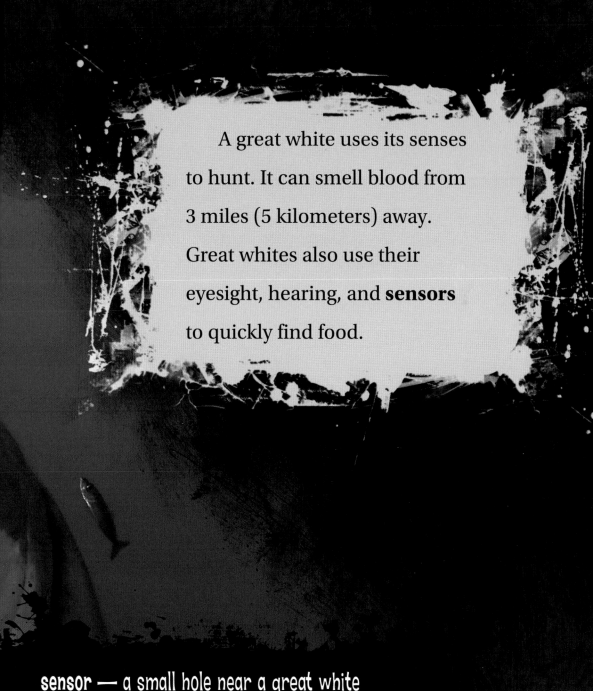

A great white uses its senses to hunt. It can smell blood from 3 miles (5 kilometers) away. Great whites also use their eyesight, hearing, and **sensors** to quickly find food.

sensor — a small hole near a great white shark's mouth

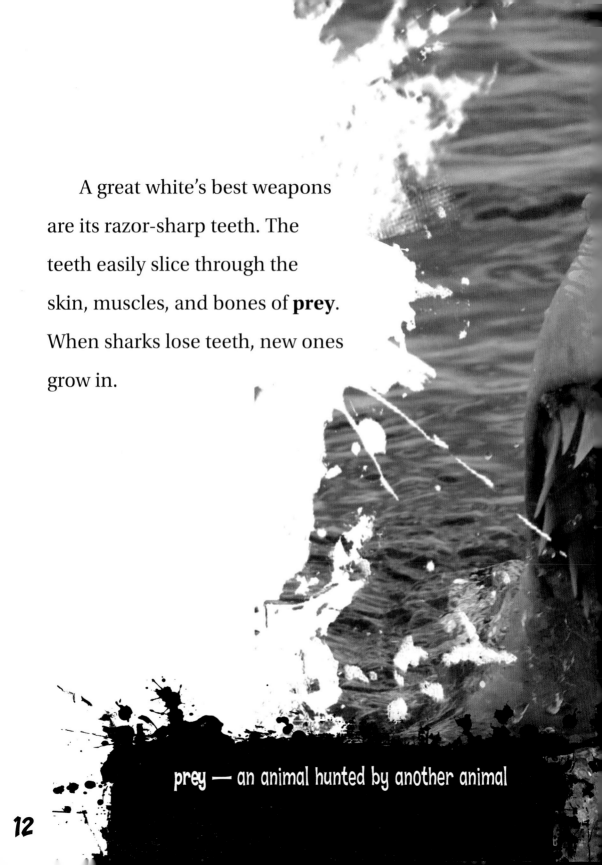

A great white's best weapons are its razor-sharp teeth. The teeth easily slice through the skin, muscles, and bones of **prey**. When sharks lose teeth, new ones grow in.

prey — an animal hunted by another animal

MAKING THE KILL

Great whites have gray backs.
Their backs help them blend in with
the ocean floor. Blending in helps
the shark sneak up on prey.

KILLER FACT

Great whites can jump as high as 6 feet
(1.8 meters) out of the water.

Great whites mostly eat sea lions, seals, and sea turtles. They also eat dead animals.

A great white quickly kills its prey. It grabs prey with its jaws. The shark then shakes its head and tears off pieces of meat.

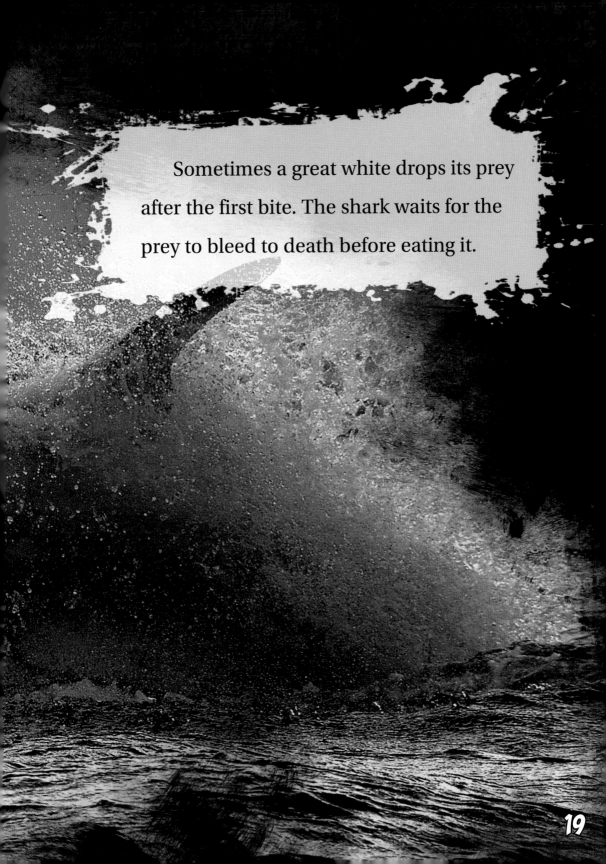

Sometimes a great white drops its prey after the first bite. The shark waits for the prey to bleed to death before eating it.

Great White Shark Diagram

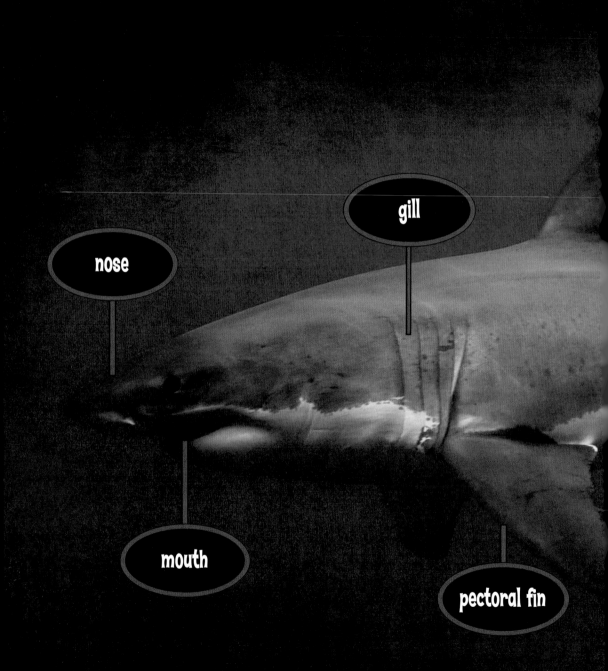

gill

nose

mouth

pectoral fin

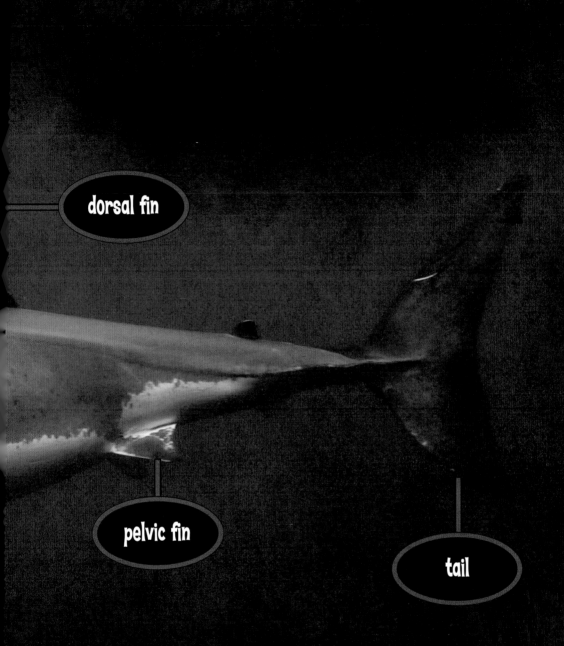

dorsal fin

pelvic fin

tail

HEADED FOR EXTINCTION?

Most people are afraid of great white sharks. But great whites don't attack people very often.

KILLER FACT

Sharks attack less than 100 people each year.

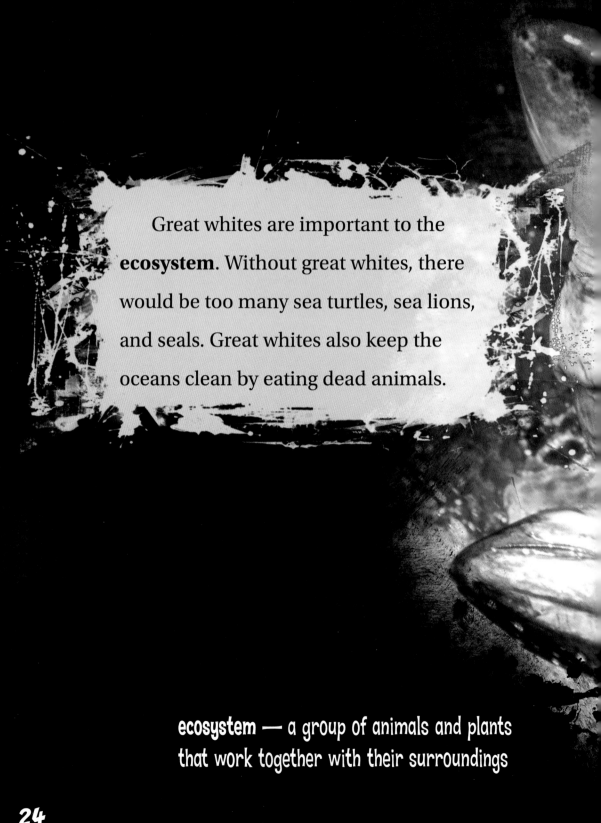

Great whites are important to the **ecosystem**. Without great whites, there would be too many sea turtles, sea lions, and seals. Great whites also keep the oceans clean by eating dead animals.

ecosystem — a group of animals and plants that work together with their surroundings

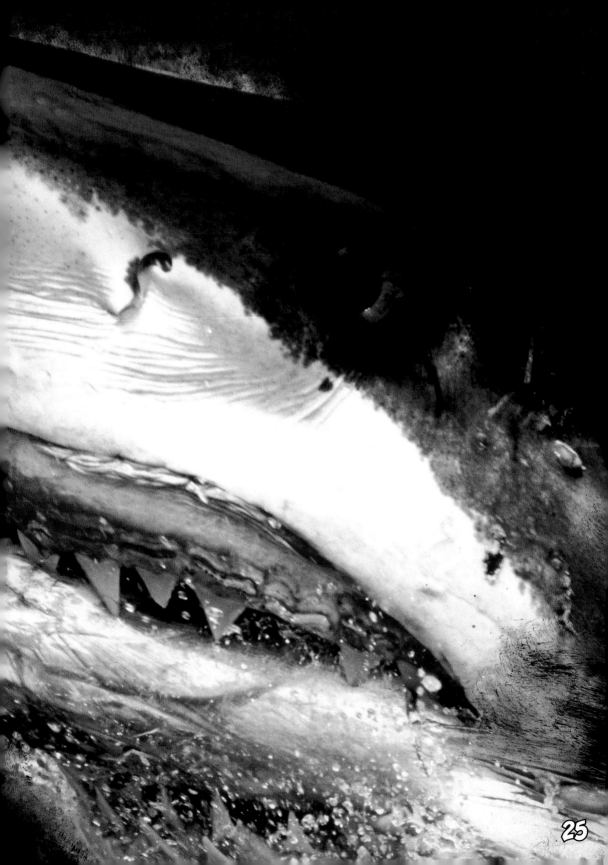

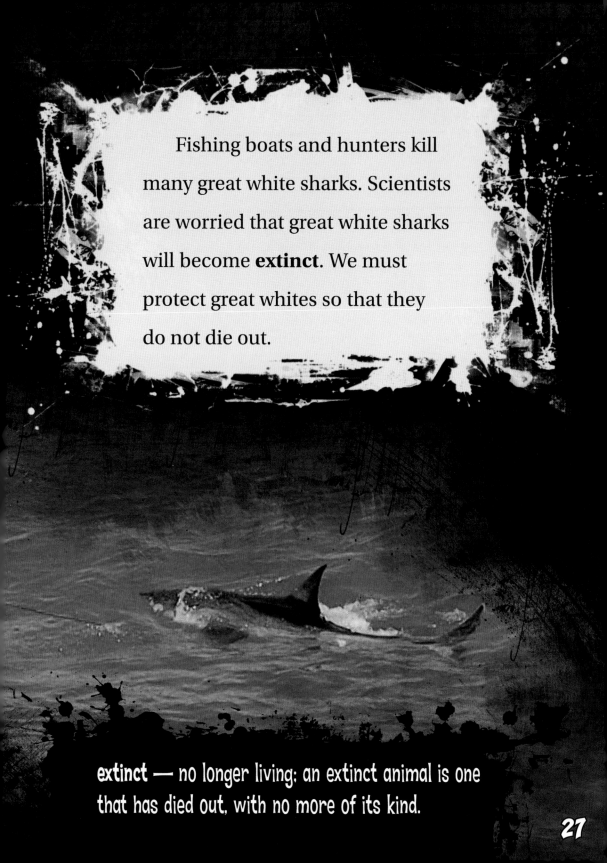

Fishing boats and hunters kill many great white sharks. Scientists are worried that great white sharks will become **extinct**. We must protect great whites so that they do not die out.

extinct — no longer living; an extinct animal is one that has died out, with no more of its kind.

Great Catch

GLOSSARY

carnivore (KAHR-nuh-vohr) — an animal that eats only meat

ecosystem (EE-koh-sis-tuhm) — a group of animals and plants that work together with their surroundings

extinct (ik-STINGKT) — no longer living; an extinct animal is one that has died out, with no more of its kind.

prey (PRAY) — an animal hunted by another animal for food

seize (SEEZ) — to take something by force

sensor (SEN-ser) — a small hole near a great white shark's mouth

slice (SLISSE) — to cut through

READ MORE

Bredeson, Carmen. *Great White Sharks Up Close.* Zoom in on Animals! Berkeley Heights, N.J.: Enslow Elementary, 2006.

Simon, Seymour. *Sharks.* New York: Collins, 2006.

Thomas, Isabel. *Shark vs. Killer Whale.* Animals Head to Head. Chicago: Raintree, 2006.

INTERNET SITES

FactHound offers a safe, fun way to find educator-approved

Internet sites related to this book.

Here's all you do:

Visit www.facthound.com

FactHound will fetch the best sites for you!

INDEX